Women in Blue

Irene Reyes-Smith

Scriptures from various versions of the Bible.

Library of Congress Cataloging – in-Publication Data has been applied for.

ISBN: 979-8-9880702-6-9

PRINTED IN THE UNITED STATES OF AMERICA.

Book Publishing Services by Pen Legacy LLC. (www.penlegacy.com)

FIRST EDITION

Table of Contents

Women in Blue

Preface

Every day, society is bombarded with images of strong men leading the charge of law enforcement in media, education, and entertainment—serving as the faces behind the badge. But no matter how often they are overlooked, thousands of women don the blue uniform, too. And their stories aren't imaginary or fabricated…these women are real.

In *Women in Blue*, Author Irene Reyes-Smith joins co-author retired Detective Victoria Woodard from Toledo, Ohio. They both come together to express and exemplify their walks of life while compiling their astounding and often heartbreaking tales of being a woman behind the badge and how it affects their lives. They are wives, mothers, sisters, daughters, and friends bound to uphold the law as they balance their lives and stressful careers. But what happens when they finally drag through the front doors of their homes after a grueling day on the streets?

…Will they even make it home?

Irene Reyes-Smith

Take the harrowing journey with ordinary women as their hearts collide with passion, pain, challenges, happiness, mountains, and valleys while simply trying to survive it all. Will they stop before they can push through all that comes at them, or will the Women in Blue use their faith in God to conquer adversity?

Acknowledgements

To my parents, Jose and Ana Reyes, who have gone on to glory. Thank you for your guidance, wisdom, encouragement, and love. Miss you, Mom and Dad.

Special thanks to my husband and best friend, Dion, for being my number one supporter and helping me during the long nights of writer's block. You are the wind beneath my wings and a blessing in my life always. Love you!

To my family and friends who have continued to believe in me and the vision that God gave me to write this story, I love you all. Many blessings.

A special thanks to Author Irene Reyes-Smith. You are such a blessing in my life. I am so grateful our paths crossed. God made this wonderful opportunity to tell my story possible through you.

To my family and friends, Maxine, Marcella, Karen, and Valerie—thanks for all the love, encouragement, and support you gave me during the process.

Irene Reyes-Smith

To Shirley Green (Ret. Lt.) Adjunct Professor at B.G.S.U. and University of Toledo, and director of the Toledo Police Museum, thank you for the many phone conversations and for sharing the women's history with me. You are one of the pioneers who helped pave the way for me and others.

We would like to acknowledge Pen Legacy for their support, assistance, and guidance in publishing this memoir, and a special thank you to Ms. Charron for her patience, positivity, and persistence in helping make this a one-of-a-kind masterpiece.

The Journey of Irene Reyes-Smith

Let me start by saying being a woman in today's society is not easy but enduring. As a 30-year retired female officer of the Metropolitan Police Department, my journey in the nation's finest police department has afforded me opportunities, challenges, and changes, along with much pain, passion, and purpose.

Not knowing what to expect, the beginning of my career was a challenge. Hearing about the crime, homicides, and dangers officers face on a day-to-day basis gave me much reason to pause. I believe people think what they see on television shows is an accurate depiction of cops, but I am here to tell you it is far from that. We deal with real-life situations in society that affect our everyday life.

Women are evolving throughout law enforcement, and it is such a positive way to show our generation of girls, teens, and young ladies that nothing or no one can hold you back from what has been destined for you to accomplish. There is a significant role in law enforcement for women of the twentieth century today because the profession was considered male-dominated. Law enforcement has allowed me to meet many people and establish many relationships—good, bad, and indifferent. I am truly thankful for the opportunity to serve the citizens, communities, and neighborhoods of the District of Columbia.

Women in law enforcement have to fight for many changes within their field, starting with the department implementing lactation rooms for breastfeeding women. This was only considered after a group of women rallied together. Before then, women would go into the ladies' restroom to pump their milk since no separate area was designated for them. We have come a long way in helping to implement change for women. Still, we have a way to go!

Another nationwide law change that occurred was giving women maternity leave so they wouldn't have to use their sick leave to be home with their newborn child. Nothing is worse than having to leave your baby to return to work only a few weeks after giving birth. And all because the job isn't willing to give women a reasonable amount of time to heal and adjust to their new stage of motherhood. Sure, the daily work operation must continue, but women should be shown some empathy while adapting to a life-altering experience, such as childbirth. Birthing a child is a blessing from the Lord, but please understand that our bodies go through major changes during and after pregnancy. And let's not mention the responsibilities of family, work schedules, and other daily duties. No, women aren't looking to receive any special privileges, but a little grace would be nice.

The Streets

I was given the opportunity to start my career as a young cadet in 1989. The program—like no other—affords young adults in high school or graduates the opportunity to start a job in their twenties and turn it into a career. It brings structure while opening your eyes to life lessons of where your life can go and what it can be.

I was so excited and grateful that someone saw a young, energetic female and assisted me on a journey to this path in my life. Being a cadet is not only the start of something great, but it lets young people know they can start something big in their life that will make a change in society and the generations to come. The cadet program allows high school students and graduates to become part of an organization helping bridge a gap between officers, communities, neighborhoods, and citizens while ensuring everyone is staying safe in a world filled with much uncertainty. We have to continue to be the mouthpiece for our youth.

Upon completing my academy training, I graduated, was sworn in, and became an officer of The Metropolitan Police Department. My career started in the Fifth District station when D.C., referred to as the Murder Capital, was at its highest crime peak in the 1990s. It was sometimes difficult keeping my ambition, drive, and curiosity high when I realized I could only help one person, one family, and one situation at a time. The crime was so intense during the 90s that work became a bit stressful, and we had to help keep each other lifted in spirit.

Policing is a unique profession that takes dedication, focus, strength, compassion, and humility. I started my career young and knew there would be some challenges but nothing I couldn't handle. The first few years were manageable. The shifts can be a bit demanding, but you find a way to keep pushing on. As women, we are resilient and sometimes act like the Energizer Bunny. We keep going and going and going, not realizing that our bodies will shut down at some point. Women are survivors, and we do what we need to do to get the job done. If I can honestly say, it's been that way with women since the beginning of time, back in the Bible days.

When women see something that needs our attention, such

as a task, situation, problem, or concern, we handle it. True, it may not always turn out like we want, but it's handled. I remember having to work sting operations, which was a real eye-opener. I often prayed to the Lord to let the task end how He desired, hopefully with no hurt, harm, or danger to anyone. In those times, I would ask myself, *why can't people just do right?*

The detail lasted through the summer months; I later went back to street patrol. I worked various details and shifts during my twelve years doing street patrol. My experiences, encounters, and energy never allowed me to get complacent. Street patrol is a compelling experience, as you never know what you will encounter. You must mentally prepare yourself for what is to come, and sometimes that's not enough.

As a woman in law enforcement, you are sized up, sometimes looked down on, and seen as a weaker vessel. But the truth is, women have prevailed in various jobs nationwide and still carry their weight today. Female officers can calm a chaotic situation by bringing the charisma, clarity, and control that is needed, but then there are times when our mouths can ignite a situation. (Hey, just being honest.) I remember responding to calls for domestic violence, family disturbances, burglaries, auto thefts, or simple assaults and saying to myself, *Lord, help me. Help me to help someone. Be with me, guide me, and protect us.*

Psalms 23:1-4 (AMP) is my favorite scripture to recite in my head: *The Lord is my Shepherd [to feed, to guide and to shield me], I shall not want. He lets me lie down in green pastures; He leads me beside the still and quiet waters. He refreshes and restores my soul (life); He leads me in the paths of righteousness for His name's sake. Even though I walk through the [sunless] valley of the shadow of death, I fear no evil, for You are with me; Your rod [to protect] and Your staff [to guide], they comfort and console me.*

We never know what we will be up against on any given

day or the outcome. While in law enforcement, you go to calls and assist citizens only to find out that you may be dealing with some of the same things in your personal life, but maybe not to the extent of what they are going through. In this profession, officers have your well-being in mind, although some people refuse to believe it. After leaving those calls when someone had to be arrested, and young children were involved and had to be taken to child protective services or turned over to the care of a family member, I often wondered how they were doing. What was the outcome? Was there anything that could have been done differently? Where are the kids now? Was the family able to work it out? So many questions, concerns, and rarely any answers.

Some of the daily patrol calls were a life-changing experience for individuals, and you wonder how you could have changed the person's perspective and helped them see a different outlook in that moment while doing what you could to help within the scope of your job. Many individuals see the uniform without understanding certain procedures are in place to help officers effectively carry out their job. Still, officers have opposition from individuals telling them how to do their job. The experiences I encountered will have you thinking about the mindset of some people and how they view the police and policing. The majority of officers would like for the public to help them be of better assistance to them. It would be great if the police and society could come to some common ground and work together. **HELP US HELP YOU!**

The Family

Family dynamics are important in the life of our young people because they see and hear so much happening today, and it all goes back to family structure. The years went by, and as a woman in law enforcement, it was no cakewalk at times. At some point in life, we all decide whether we want to start a family or not. I became a mother to two healthy, wonderful children. The birth of my kids gave me a broader outlook on life. Thinking about raising two kids would be while being a single mom with a demanding job, I knew it wouldn't be easy. Still, I believe in the power of prayer.

What God gives, He also provides for, and children are a blessing from the Lord. While the kids were young, I had my family's support. I tell all mothers don't think you have to do it alone. Parenting is a ministry. You have to take time to nurture, care, shape, and guide your children so they can be effective and eager to want the best out of life, which is what God promises to us.

With any demanding profession, you need all the help you can get. This was especially true for me while working in the nation's capital. With the magnitude of parades, concerts, and other events, law enforcement officers had to be prepared to respond at a moment's notice. The days can be long, and you have to prepare your mind to deal with unforeseen situations in unpredictable weather— cold nights, hot days, snow, and sleet. I guess you can say I imagined something a little different than what I experienced. The challenges were becoming more real now. So, would I continue in this profession or find something more conducive to my situation as a single parent? A firm believer that anything I put my mind to I will complete effectively, I pressed forward.

Now twelve years in, it was getting harder and more hectic. My kids' lives were upside down, and my son was not adapting well to me having to work different shifts. He especially didn't like staying with family and friends so much while I worked. I began praying and seeking God during this time of turmoil. Some days, I cried myself to sleep. I remember God's word: *Weeping may endure for a night, but THE Joy of the Lord comes in the morning.* I heard God's voice say, *do not fear, for I am with you: Don't be discouraged, for I am your God. I will strengthen you and help you.* **Isaiah 41:10 (NLT)** God was my guide!

As women, we are taught to be strong and often don't speak on all the things we juggle on a daily basis: kids, careers, households, and more. We endure despite being tired, in pain, or mentally exhausted. I remember having a conversation with my mother about everything and what I should do about it.

"Baby, pray about it," she told me. "God will show you. Listen to His response because He makes all things possible."

I did just that, and the Lord opened the door for me to be switched to an inside position with a schedule that would allow me to be with my kids more.

I truly enjoyed my job and the opportunities it afforded me. I was even able to purchase my first home. What a great accomplishment! The kids were excited, and the joy I saw on their faces was enough for me to say to myself, *what a wonderful God I serve! Nothing is too hard for my God to handle.* The law enforcement field is one where many times you bring the job home because it doesn't STOP! People are calling you about one question or another. You're being emailed about lock-ups, property, a situation, or a call you went to that day or earlier in the week. An officer's mind is always processing something, which I'm not sure is good or bad. One thing is for sure—you are constantly on guard.

The Silence

Women in policing sometimes suffer in silence. We go through so much with our bodies after childbirth, handle so much mentally, and endure in a male-dominant profession. As we all know, policing involves working the streets to patrol communities and neighborhoods. I remember an incident when I became pregnant with my first child and had to start working an inside position.

One day, a male sergeant told me, "Some women need not do this job because all they want to do is get pregnant and work inside." I was appalled and hurt by his comment, but having only five years on the job, I didn't know what to say or want to go up against my superior. So, I let it go. Time passed, but that statement stayed with me. Still, I never told anyone. That same sergeant would walk around making irritating and obnoxious comments about pregnant female officers until I'd finally had enough. One day, I said to him, "I don't think you should be making comments about officers getting pregnant because you came from a woman." He stood there speechless as I continued. "I'm sure you have females in your family who has had kids and had to modify their work schedules. Furthermore, without a woman, there would be no you." I didn't have any more issues with him after that.

Women have to stick together and stand up for themselves. Some men make the mistake of thinking we won't respond to their sarcasm. That encounter made me wonder if that's how some men really view women, or was that just *his* way of thinking? We must change the office environment of the workforce, corporations, and government so women will not have to endure opposition, unfair treatment, unreasonable pay, and stressful situations on the job. I still believe the word of God, which says, *no weapon formed against me shall prosper, and every tongue that rises against me will be condemned.* His word is true and never fails us. The Lord reminds me in **Psalms 139:13-14 (HCSB):** *For it was You who created my inward parts; You knit me together in my mother's womb. I will praise You because I have been remarkably and wonderfully made. Your works are wonderful, and I know this very well.*

I encourage every woman to follow your dreams, aspirations, and goals while knowing God makes provisions for all the visions, He gives you. He is with us every step of the way. Women have come a long way and are now speaking up regarding their mental state, well-being, and life purpose. In life, there are times when God will fight for us and times when He will instruct us to be silent. The scripture that comes to mind is **Exodus 14:14** (**AMP**): The Lord will fight for you while you [only need to] keep silent *and* remain calm.

My Purpose

Law enforcement is like no other profession. It's one of the few jobs where not having your head in it can result in harm or death to someone or even yourself, depending on the situation. My children were my life, and becoming a mother was the best thing to ever happen to me. The job was the beginning of what God had instilled in me to guide and assist. Life can throw you curveballs, and you must figure out which ones you'll catch and which you'll let fall to the ground. Without the trials and tribulations, I encountered during this journey, I wouldn't have had the opportunity to write this book based on my experiences that will hopefully help someone else along the way. God has a purpose for us all, and His timing is always right.

MPDC was a family away from home. You develop many friendships, some closer than others. We are indeed *my brother's and my sister's keeper,* as the Bible says. I believe we all have a purpose, and we must follow our purpose to fulfill what our maker in heaven has placed in us. As a woman in law enforcement, we live and work in a world where women are breaking ceilings by rising to the occasion but still coming up against opposition. The everyday trials, tests, and tasks for women in law enforcement take a toll on us, but we were made to be resilient from the beginning of time. Women are the glue that holds a lot of things together. We can put a smile on our faces, all the while being stressed, suffering, and fighting to survive. Yes, we all have decisions and choices to make in life, but we must remember to stay the course and know that *only what we do for Christ will last.* So many thoughts and questions run through my mind, some of which remain unanswered and leave me wondering.

Irene Reyes-Smith

Questions I've often asked myself:

- Is there anything I would have done differently in my career?

- Is there a situation or outcome with someone that could have been handled differently?

- Will the person I arrested come out a changed person after this? Or will their arrest begin an unimaginable life for them?

Women in law enforcement are unique. Not only do they raise their children, take care of their household, and care for family members, but they also nurture and guide the youth and serve as mentors and role models. Being a police officer, you must understand your role, be ready for any and everything, and remember that what you do, say, or react can leave a lasting impression on someone. At the beginning of your career, those things are not always your focus. However, after a few years on the job, you realize just how big these factors play in your success as an officer.

Lessons Learned

The memoir *Women in Blue* came from a vision that the Lord gave me to acknowledge women in a profession they were told was a man's job, but women can accomplish the same goals as anyone. Women are often victims of disrespect, unfair treatment, and sexual overtones, but we hide our feelings well. The reality is women are needed in this world.

I remember being on the streets and praying before going to calls—whether it was domestic violence, a family disturbance, a man with a gun, a missing person, or a simple assault. I would say to myself, *Lord, be with us. You know the situation at hand. Go before me and calm the matter. Let the individuals know that all will be well and You are with them and protect us.* We never know what we will be up against on a given day or the outcome. Yes, officers are to protect and serve, but when you need to call the police for help or assistance, remember officers are human, too. They are the ones who answer the call and put their life on the line when they step up to do their job. The Bible says, *many are called, but few are chosen.* That is still true today because not everyone can do this profession called Policing, but everyone will always have an opinion of how things should be.

Policing is the profession that has the authority to change someone's life entirely. The Bible says in **Romans 13:5** (**AMP**): *Therefore, one must be subject [to civil authorities], not only to escape the punishment [that comes with wrongdoing], but also as a matter of principle [knowing what is right before God].* My experience in policing will live with me forever. No matter where you go or what you do after being an officer of the law, it will stick with you. The job makes a huge impact on you and your family's life. How you think about things is different, your influence on lives is different, your interaction with individuals is different, and your awareness is heightened. You feel like you can't be yourself like other individuals because you are held to different standards even though you are human.

Policing is a profession where everyone wants to think they can do your job better than you, not understanding the guidelines, laws, policies, and procedures that must be followed. The job is one where officers run to the fight while others run away. An average individual will have a hard time wrapping their mind around that concept, but officers understand that risks come with the profession. Female officers are often treated disrespectfully by citizens and communities but do their job as well as, if not better than, their male counterparts. A woman's intuition kicks in and goes the extra mile on the job, ensuring the situation, circumstances, issues, and tasks at hand are resolved promptly and professionally.

Don't Count Women Out!

The profession has also allowed me to soar and achieve my goals in life. I remember joining The National Black Police Association (NBPA) in Washington, DC. I became the first African American woman with a Hispanic heritage background to be the vice president of the DC Chapter. The organization allowed officers from all over to network and gain more insight into other departments' operations. I remember while serving in that capacity, other law enforcement women would inquire how they could join and be the change that society, communities, and organizations needed. The organization's main goal was to ensure that justice and injustice throughout the departments were carried out fairly and proportionally manner among African American officers and in the communities they patrolled. Several other law enforcement organizations have also been established, such as NOBLE (National Organization of Black Women in Law Enforcement) and the International Council of Women in Law Enforcement, to name a few.

*London, England, with the England Officers
National Black Police Association Conference*

Irene Reyes-Smith

Psalms 37:23 (AMP): *The steps of a [good and righteous] man are directed and established by the Lord, And He delights in his way [and blesses his path].* This scripture would come to mind while working. God was with me every step of my journey—the good times, bad situations, ugly encounters, and praise reports. I ask myself, *If God has given us the power we need, why do we sometimes feel powerless?* We can discuss many professions and careers, but none compare to policing. The women that get up every day and put on the uniform to protect life, preserve it, and patrol the communities are not always commended for the job they do. I understand it is a choice to work whatever job or career you choose, but someone has to do it. The fact that policing is in the public's eye makes it the most critiqued, criticized, and critical job. Every now and then, some do express their gratitude by saying, "Thank you, Officer," or "Job well done," or "Glad you're here." Just remember, your words of thanks help remind an officer why they chose their profession.

The experiences and encounters throughout my career have taught me that no matter your status, profession, or outlook in life, without the Word of God guiding you and keeping you on the path He sets before you, what is it all for? Women have come a long way but still have more to do. Women in blue are genuine and hardworking, putting others first as they commit to the cause of their profession. Both men and women play a part in today's society, each having an obligation and a role to fulfill. God created us all in His image and said it was good. So, no one individual is better or more powerful than another. I often think back to Martin Luther King Jr.'s speech, "I Have a Dream" … You know the rest.

The Journey of
Victoria Woodard

Born in Toledo, Ohio, in the fall of 1955, I grew up in the 800 block of Belmont Avenue, where its residents were made up of working, middle-class, diverse families. Nine commercial businesses were between the 600 block at Ewing Street and the 900 block at N. Hawley Street. Directly across the street from our house was a beauty and barber shop connected to a bar owned by a brother and sister. We knew all our neighbors because they were a part of our "village ", and if we got out of line, our "village" would correct us without having any fear of repercussions from our parents.

Having eight siblings—three sisters and five brothers—our family was considered large back then. There was always a lot of laughter and pranks played on the girls by the boys, and music played a major role in our lives, even today. We were even encouraged to take music lessons. You would hear some form of music in the house daily. We owned a piano and organ, plus we brought home our instruments from school. The only instrument off-limits was our father's acoustic guitar. On Saturdays, we cleaned the house while listening to gospel albums. The best part of living directly across from the bar, especially in the summertime and on weekends, was the endless music that only stopped long enough for the patrons to feed more quarters into the jukebox. On school nights, my mother would yell up the stairs for us to close the window. She never knew we only closed it halfway. Many nights after dinner, my father would tell one of us to go get his guitar. Then he would play and sing the Blues as he sat in his La-Z-Boy while we sat at his feet egging him on and making requests.

Straining to listen to the constant chatter from her police scanner, my mother would look over at him and give him the side-eye. I remember only hearing male voices coming from the scanner that she listened to religiously.

Located exactly four houses down from our house, on the same side of the street, stood a red metal box that required a key to open it. Written across its locked door were raised letters that spelled out **Police Telegraph**. The box was attached to a pole on a pedestal that was about six feet tall. As a child, I had no idea what the purpose was for this red box. All I know is no child in the area messed with it. Every child in the neighborhood must have been given the same "You better not touch it" speech regarding the red box. It was never climbed on, played around, or defaced. We respected that red box. Many years later, I learned the connection of the red box— known as a Police Officer Callbox—to my mother's scanner. Only God knew that the little girl from Belmont Avenue would one day return to that same corner as one of Toledo's Finest.

As a child, I loved to ask a lot of questions. I needed to know the answers to questions everyone else was too afraid to ask. I paid attention to details and enjoyed solving mysteries. After high school, I decided to pursue a college education, majoring in Elementary Education to teach English. However, as time went on, I felt unsure of my goal in life. By now, it was the early 80s, and the city of Toledo announced its plan to hire the largest number of officers ever in 1983. I decided to throw my hat in the ring.

After completing the hiring process and taking the Civil Service Exam, all I had left to do was wait. When I received the call from the recruitment staff telling me that I had been accepted into the police academy, I was ecstatic. Only thirty-five people had been selected. I actually thought I was being pranked and had to confirm the conversation to be sure. Immediately, I informed my mother of my new career. Needless to say, she was not happy with my choice since she wanted me to attend beauty school to become a hairdresser. My uncle K.C. had even offered to pay for it. I don't recall my mother listening to her police scanner ever again after that day. My father, on the other hand, was proud as ever. My mother wanted me to be who she wanted me to be, but I had to be who God called me to be.

After all my excitement died down, I thought about what it would mean to become an officer of the law. I had no clue what the job entailed, but I was up for the challenge and determined to forge ahead. Before the start of the Academy, I began running to get in shape for the physical training, and I'm so glad I did. I was in the best shape of my life by graduation time.

The 39th Toledo Police Academy Class

My journey began on September 7, 1984. The thirty-five recruits were divided into four squads with alphabetical seating. I was in the fourth squad, seated in the fourth row in the last seat. As I looked around the room, no one looked familiar, but we all had the same scared "fish out of water" look on our faces. Seated next to me was a black male identified as Perry Waddell. He drove an Eldorado Cadillac that looked around thirty feet long. He was extremely nice and kind to everyone.

Irene Reyes-Smith

We started a friendship that has lasted for thirty-nine years now.

Academy Staff asked the new trainees to stand one at a time to introduce themselves and state why they wished to become an officer. Some recruits responded with the usual reply of wanting to make the world a better place or helping the community. I sat there thinking, *What a load of crap!* When it was finally my time to speak, I talked about the positions I would strive for—one being a dispatcher. Back then, only men who were "seasoned" police officers became dispatchers, not civilians. The staff of men looked at me and smiled. Then one of them stated, "Trainee Woodard, I'm afraid you're going to have to grow whiskers for that." That response took the wind out of my sails. I didn't know how to respond, so I didn't.

An hour before dismissal, we were ordered to change into our Physical Training (PT) issued t-shirt and shorts. We were going outside to exercise and run one mile. The shorts were so short it looked like we were wearing Daisy Dukes. It wasn't a good look on the women and looked even worse on the men. We didn't care because we just wanted to get it over with.

An hour later, we were dismissed. I remember walking to my car, carrying everything issued to me that day. Physically tired and mentally exhausted, I asked myself, *what have you gotten yourself into?* There was no turning back now, though. The following day, a staff member informed the class that a recruit had dropped out. He decided he would rather join a band that played punk rock music. At this point, even I was questioning my decision.

After being fitted for uniforms, it never occurred to me that they were men's uniforms. I remember seeing women hired before me wearing the winter uniform, and the cuffs on their shirts and jackets were turned up rather than tailored to fit. I, too, was fitted for men's uniforms. The polyester double-knit pants were a straight cut, which posed a problem for a black girl with hips. I was swimming in the oversized shirts with their long tails tucked into my pants. Everything had to be tailored. It took weeks to get it all done. No matter how many times I had uniforms altered, they still didn't fit. The only good thing about wearing male shirts was the pockets. They were large enough to hold my notepad, and I could easily get my hands in and out of them. Some of us were even wearing men's boots. The shoes for the ladies were just as bad. We had two choices—plain black leather lace-up or patented leather lace-up, with no tread on the bottoms. During Physical Training (PT), they made us run an obstacle course and do sprints in full uniform, wearing those slick bottom shoes. It wasn't until several years later that women were finally fitted for female uniforms. Some women preferred to continue wearing the altered male shirts, again for pocket space. As for myself, I alternated between men's and women's shirts for the next ten years while on patrol.

The Ride Along

I was determined to hang in there and finish what I started. Before completion of the Academy and right before graduation, we had to go on what is called the Ride Along. Recruits are paired with "seasoned" officers who show the "rookies" the ropes while working in patrol.

I reported to the Central District Station roll call room. The room was an ample open space with tables and chairs, which was intimidating but not as much as the big men seated at those tables. They laughed and talked amongst themselves until the Command announced, "Attention to Roll Call!" Looking around the room, I wondered which one of the men would be my partner for the day. As names and assignments were called, it was apparent some of the seasoned officers were not happy to be split apart from their regular crew and partners. The officer I was paired with did not engage me unless necessary.

It was now lunchtime, and we ate in silence at a local restaurant. I didn't mind him not talking to me because I was focused on listening to my radio, not wanting to miss a call. We didn't have computers in the cars and paddy wagons back then, so our radios were our only lines of communication. When it was time to pay the bill, my partner realized he didn't have enough money to cover his expenses. Smiling, I offered to pay the difference. I couldn't wait to return to class the next day and share my experience. My experience was better than another Black female's experience. I was still determined not to let this stop me from hitting the streets of Toledo as a Certified Police Officer. This new adventure I was about to embark on just became real. So, I decided to choose my faith over fear.

Graduation day was upon us, and the anticipation of being an officer was exciting and scary at the same time. Six months later, I was assigned to the graveyard shift. It took its toll on my body, and I was sleep-deprived many nights.

In 1984, Field Training Officers (FTO) did not exist. So, seasoned officers willing to share his wisdom were paired with us. I say "his" wisdom because the shift was made up mainly of men. Yes, more females were on the job, just not on this shift. Some men did not care for the new changes and didn't hide their displeasure and resistance. There were even cases of the "Blue Flu," where they chose to go home sick rather than work with a rookie or a woman.

I was fortunate enough to work with a seasoned officer eager to share his knowledge with me. We were an Inner-City Wagon Crew and stayed busy all night responding to calls. He was an adrenaline junkie and loved recovering stolen vehicles with the driver still inside. I was eager to learn, and he was eager to teach me. I especially liked the fact that I was policing the neighborhood where I grew up. I knew the community and its residents, and they knew me. What an honor it was to *Protect and Serve* those citizens. To me, police work is not hard, but I will say it's tough. We have to be many things to many people. It takes a lot of patience, compassion, understanding, prayer, and common sense. It can be very stressful at times and a thankless job most of the time.

As I looked around Central District Station, I saw that many female officers held positions inside. While researching information for this book, I discovered that if you were a female hired prior to 1982, there was a good chance you were behind a desk. Most female officers in the early years were assigned to investigate women and children's crimes only. These women were members of what was known as the Women's Bureau. I always heard stories about three Black women (early hires) who paved the way. There is a police photo that shows them dressed classy in their Sunday best. The first Black female was hired in 1922, and the second and third in 1946.

In 1976, Retired Lieutenant Shirley Green and Retired Detective Debra Woodard (no relation) were the first class of women to "hit the street" in patrol. This only occurred because women had started to file lawsuits over their classification as policewomen versus police officers. Policewomen assigned to the Juvenile Bureau in 1976 now had the choice of working in patrol and making the same pay as men or remaining behind a desk. If you were a female hired in the 37th Academy Class in 1982, this was the last class of women to take the police test known as the Police Women's Test. The department was no longer segregated by gender, according to Shirley Green (Ret. Lt.), who was the only Black female in a Command position and head of the Juvenile Bureau at the time. She is the first female, Black or White, to reach the rank of lieutenant. Because of rotation, I did not see Lt. Green until I worked the day shift. To help me understand the department's history, I joined the Afro-American Patrolmen's League (AAPL) and eventually became the president of the Toledo Chapter. I remained president for many years during my career.

Irene Reyes-Smith

As told to me by Retired Officer Sneed, the Toledo Chapter was formed in 1968 to handle problems unique to Black officers. This organization introduced me to the National Black Police Association (NBPA), which offered yearly training and education classes. I earned over 800 hours of additional training and college credits through this training. I was very impressed with both organizations and proud to be a part of them.

Finally, I had enough seniority to hold a spot on the afternoon shift. I enjoyed working between the hours of 2:30 p.m. to 10:30 p.m. If you like to stay busy, this is the shift for you since it is usually fast-paced and full of action. I loved staying busy, so I was in heaven. I didn't mind taking call after call. It made the time go by faster.

Police work is like a box of chocolates—you never knew what you would get. When I became permanent on the afternoon shift, I was assigned to a regular wagon crew with a partner. I was excited for two reasons. I was working a paddy wagon, which was my preference, and patrolling in my old childhood neighborhood. It was a win-win situation for me. I loved working with a wagon crew. My partner and I were go-getters who took our job seriously and were well-respected in the community. We worked very well together, taking care of our district and its citizens.

The longer you work together, the more you get to know your partner. In some cases, you know your partner better than your spouse. You become close because, as an officer, we never know when the "grits are going to hit the fan." My partner and I used a lot of non-verbal communication when we felt a situation was about to go left. We depended on each other to stay alert and alive. We were involved in many situations that left one of us with a minor injury. There were many times God protected us from grave danger.

I recall one incident when my partner and I were dispatched to a domestic violence call. Upon our arrival, a male Caucasian answered the door and stated, "I don't want any n***** cops. I want some White cops." The dispatcher was advised of what the complainant said, but hearing the other individual inside screaming, we pushed past the complainant to assess the situation despite his racial comments. The complainant then charged us with a tire iron, swinging it at us as he quickly approached. We pulled our weapons, and he immediately dropped it. I didn't think about it then, but as you're driving home, the realization that one or both of us could have lost our lives or been forced to take someone else's life sinks in. I thanked God we lived another day to talk about it.

I remember the stress I experienced while being sued for excessive force. I was working alone and was dispatched to a call that involved an alleged suspect armed with a sawed-off shotgun inside a residence. My lawsuit involved a person who inserted himself into police business. As I approached the area, I saw him walking in the middle of the road. He was warned several times to leave the area of the man who was said to have a gun but refused. As I waited for backup, the male continued to approach me. I opened my car door and placed my left foot on the ground while informing the dispatcher of what was occurring. The whole time I continued telling him to leave. Instead of following my orders, he grabbed the car door and pressed it against my lower leg to stop me from getting out of the car. Backup arrived just in time, and we attempted to place the male under arrest, who struggled and resisted. Due to the icy road conditions, we all fell into a nearby ditch while still struggling with him. Keep in mind the initial call I was dispatched to was also still happening. Situations like this are extremely dangerous for an officer because we have to shift our focus from one life-threatening situation to another.

I didn't report to work the following day because just above my ankle was injured, and my body hurt from falling into the ditch. Imagine falling on your back while wearing heavy equipment and having the weight of another man land on top of you. Painful indeed.

Several weeks later, I was informed through a written complaint filed that I was being sued by the individual who assaulted me. The lawsuit named me as the arresting officer who inflicted serious bodily harm on him. If that were the case, he would have been refused at the Lucas County Jail until he received treatment at the hospital. He was booked without injuries. He listed several bogus injuries, of which he did not seek medical attention. The complaint also stated he would need therapy due to his injuries. Not only did he want a cash settlement, but he also wanted to take my car and house from me. I couldn't believe what I was reading. I knew I didn't do the things he accused me of, but it was still stressful. During the lengthy internal investigation, it was discovered that this lawsuit was not his first rodeo. He had a prior history of filing lawsuits against other police officers, hoping that one of them would result in a cash settlement. I thanked God that the weapon formed against me did not prosper.

Community Services Officer

Crime and gangs were on the rise in the community and our school system. As President of the Afro-American Patrolmen's League, a decision was made to do our part with helping to stop the violence. We came up with the idea of a basketball camp for the youth. It provided a positive outlet and was well received. We called it the Stop the Violence Campaign. In September of 1994, the AAPL was presented with a proclamation from the Office of the Mayor, and September officially became known as the "Stop the Violence and Save our Youth" month.

Because of all the violence within the school system, the police department developed a Community Services section. Officers were stationed inside junior high and high schools on a full-time basis. I was chosen as a School Resource Officer

(SRO) and assigned to a junior high school that was gang infested with both male and female members. There were seven identified gangs inside my school. I had no problem identifying them because they wore their colors with pride, and the girl gangs were more violent than the boys. I had to conduct random weapon searches. I had my hands full and prayed every day that the gang violence, which mostly occurred outside after school, didn't spill over on the inside.

Not only was I responsible for this school but also eight Feeder schools around me. Many days, I was called to one or more of the Feeder schools to handle problems. Once, I had a second-grade student bring 30-06 ammunition to school for Show and Tell. He told me it belonged to his father. Something had to be done, but what?

At my school, I had a male student who was heavily involved in gangs but didn't attend school promptly show up at dismissal to cause problems. I engaged him every time I saw him and dealt with him accordingly. I would always make it a point to say to him, "You are headed to one of two places—prison or the cemetery. "Our interactions like this went on for months.

In the meantime, the Department sent me to a week-long training class put on by the Federal Law Enforcement Training Center (FLETC) in Glycol, Georgia, called the G.R.E.A.T. Program (Gang Resistance Education and Training), a school-based, police-officer-instructed program. After returning to school, I would instruct a different lesson or drills that would give needed skills on avoiding gangs and violence. Some students were receptive, and others not so much.

Wanting to also focus on the kids doing the right thing, I came up with a friendly competition between the elementary and junior high students. My elementary schools would compete for the least tardiness and best attendance, while my junior high schools would compete for the best grades. After listening to kids complain about the school lunch, I contacted the local fast-food restaurants—McDonald's and Burger King—and asked for their participation in recognizing my schools' most improved students with a complimentary meal. Both restaurants did not hesitate to support my program. The students were chosen once a month by me. I named the elementary school program the *Battle for the Burger* and the junior high program the *Lunch Bunch*. The kids loved it, and it was a tremendous success. Attendance, grades, and tardiness all improved.

I was still instructing my class on gangs. Sadly, all the gang training in the world meant nothing to the kids who lived their lives surrounded by negative influence and violence every day. The class was almost laughable to the kids involved in gangs. I didn't give up, though. If I could get to one student, it would be good enough for me. One day, I noticed that the young male gangbanger I mentioned earlier was coming inside the school and going to classes. He became my most improved student. I knew a cheeseburger, fries, and a shake wasn't going to change lives, but it was a start.

I wanted students to experience what college life is like. So, I contacted Bowling Green State University (BGSU) and scheduled a tour. I encouraged the young male gangbanger to come along. The university treated them to a free lunch at the end. I had great success with everyone I reached out to; my students had a "village." My programs did so well that the young gangbanger turned his life around. His success story was featured in our local newspaper, *The Toledo Blade*. The mayor's office wrote a letter to the chief's office on my behalf, thanking me for a job well done. My prayers were answered. My job became less stressful because of the relationship between the police and the students. I remained a School Resource Officer for the next four years.

In late 1997, the Department started the Officer Exchange Program, allowing an officer to work temporarily in the position of their choice for one month. I enjoyed working with the students but also wanted to shadow a female detective, one of the early hires assigned to the Juvenile Bureau. Her experience was with crimes committed by juveniles, and I felt having additional knowledge couldn't hurt. So, I submitted my bid, which was accepted, to do the job of a detective in the Investigative Services Bureau.

The first week was spent shadowing the detective. To my surprise, I was on my own the second week. I was given an unmarked Plymouth K-Car to drive and my first case to investigate. I was used to interviewing juveniles but had no experience dealing with a juvenile victim of sexual assault committed by an adult. After speaking to the victim and witnesses, it was time to find the alleged suspect. After locating where he worked, I contacted him and scheduled an interview over the phone. When he told me he couldn't keep his appointment because he didn't have transportation, I suggested he find a ride or I would come to him. He never asked why I wanted to talk to him or what it was about. On the day of his interview, he showed up on a bicycle.

I began the interview process and started my line of questioning. Then I suddenly remembered I needed to record it. We used VHS tapes back then. So, I excused myself and went to the lieutenant's office, where the VHS recorder was located. When I entered the room, all the seasoned male detectives and the lieutenant were there watching and listening to the interview, which I had no idea they were doing. "Get back in there. You're doing great! " one of them said after putting the tape in the machine for me.

Before going back inside the interview room, I whispered a prayer and asked the Lord to give me the words to say. I continued the interview, that quickly turned into an interrogation. The alleged suspect gave his confession, which he described in detail. After only seven days of receiving the case, I cleared it with an arrest, and the violator is currently serving a life sentence. The seasoned detectives complimented me on my interview technique and skills. They admitted they had doubted I could solve the case. Their compliments meant a lot to me, especially since they were the "heavy hitters".

After that case, I was sent out with a seasoned detective who primarily investigated homicide cases. I enjoyed those cases and the knowledge I gained from them. Once the month was over, I returned to the junior high school.

In the meantime, a bid opened for a detective position in the Investigative Services Bureau. I submitted my bid, then went on vacation. I just knew I didn't stand a chance. I felt this way because there wasn't a female in the Investigative Services Bureau who looked like me. After my return to work, to my surprise, after returning to work, I was scheduled for an interview. I knew I would make an excellent detective and was ready to be interviewed. Bring it on!

The interview process was twofold. It started with Command Officers asking about the duties of a detective. Looking at their faces as I answered their questions, I sensed I was on the right track. During the second half, I was placed inside an empty room and given a written scenario. It described a crime scene that was filled with several twists and turns. My job was to read the scenario and then write in detail the type of crime being committed, the person committing it, and what I would do as the Lead Investigator to solve it. I read the scenario three times because it didn't make sense to me. I would start writing and then stop. I had three pieces of balled-up paper in front of me. Not being a quitter, I was determined to figure it out. Suddenly, it was as if a switch was turned on inside my brain. I began writing my answer in detail and knew I had nailed it.

Weeks later, I was informed I was being assigned to the Investigative Services Bureau as of October 1, 1998. I immediately told the school principal that I had a new assignment. Every day before the dismissal bell, I would go outside and sit in my car to keep an eye on the buses.

Unbeknownst to me, the principal announced over the PA system that it was my last day. When the bell rang, the kids busted through the doors and ran over to my patrol car, surrounding it. "Get on the bus!" I shouted at them, not knowing why they rushed to me. Some had tears in their eyes and started crying. They wanted to know why I was leaving. I tried to explain, but they weren't trying to hear it. Some students missed their bus, but they didn't care. In that moment, I could see and feel how the students truly felt about me. My prayers were answered. I just wanted them to prosper and do well. They realized I was human underneath the blue uniform, just like them. They knew that Officer Woodard cared about them. As for the kids who missed their bus, I loaded them into my car and drove them home. It was the least I could do. Many times, I questioned my purpose in life. That day, it became crystal clear to me that the little girl from Belmont Avenue has the ability to change the lives of other little girls and boys.

In 1998 when I became a detective, there was no separation between crimes committed against persons and crimes against property. You just did the job. It wasn't broken down into titles like it is today. Whatever case came in, that's what you were assigned. Sometime later, the two sections were separated. Unlike larger cities, Toledo Police had no homicide unit or detectives that only handled homicide cases. You worked as a team. All detectives received the same training. It wasn't until after I retired that a Cold Case Unit was formed. Back then, you served at the Chief's discretion. Sometimes you were pulled from your assignment to work on an undercover assignment. The Vice Narcotics Unit used me for two days to go undercover and make drug buys from a known drug dealer. Believe me, it's nothing like television. The sale could happen quickly or play out for hours. In this case, it was hours and hours and hours. I found it to be boring and scary at the same time. It was scary because you didn't know if the Confidential Informant (C.I.) would turn on you and blow your cover.

Irene Reyes-Smith

I had so many cases open that I had to take my laptop—which was thick as a brick—home to keep up. At the end of the month, all that matters is the case's disposition. Investigative work doesn't end after your eight-hour shift is over. Sometimes it goes on for days, months, and even years.

I remained in Investigative Services, wearing many different hats for the next fifteen years until retirement. While gathering information for this book, I discovered I was the first African American woman to become a detective assigned to the Investigative Services Bureau. Unlike the early hires, I competed against male officers for the position in a post-gender segregated era. What God has for me is for me. I had a wonderful career. It didn't feel like work to me. I enjoyed it, and God kept me through it all. I now know what a brotherhood is and what it feels like to be a part of one. I consider it an honor to be a member of the Law Enforcement Family.

Investigative Services Unit of Toledo, Ohio

Irene Reyes-Smith

As law enforcement officers, we witness many things that others only see in nightmares or movies. On some occasions, the situations made me laugh, but I'm the type of person who can find humor in just about anything. I look at laughter as a gift from God. It certainly got me through a lot of stressful days. Allow me to share three of my favorite memories.

My First Foot Pursuit

My academy class was off probation and released to work on our own. I was assigned that day to work on the Eastside of Toledo with a fellow classmate. Unless you grew up there and knew the one-way streets, you could get turned around. Neither of us knew the area, and back then, we didn't have GPS or computers in cars. We used the Graphic Street Guide, which meant we had to look it up.

It was a hot sunny day, and everyone was outside. My partner and I observed a male known to have a felony warrant for his arrest walking down the street. When he saw us, he fled on foot. We jumped out of the car, now in pursuit of him. He was all over the place—running between houses, down alleyways, then back on the street again. We looked like a chase scene from those old black-and-white Keystone Cops films. Briefly, we lost sight of him between houses. While searching one street over, we saw a lady running from out of a house like she was on fire.

"Get that man out of my house!" she screamed, waving her arms frantically.

He was so desperate to get away from us that he ran up to her front door, which was open, and dashed inside. We entered the house, and there he was—tired and sweaty from running––sitting on her sofa with his legs crossed and pretending to watch television.

With a straight face, he looked at us and said, "I live here."

After we stopped laughing, he went to jail.

Everything Isn't for Everybody

There was this young lady, and whenever I saw her, she would ask about my job as a police officer. She felt she could do the job. So, I suggested she go through the process of riding along with me for an eight-hour shift to see firsthand what we do. Once she agreed, she was cleared by the Department to ride along on a Friday. I was working the afternoon shift, which was full of action. So, she was definitely going to see something up close and personal.

As soon as we entered the patrol car, I heard the familiar tone coming through the radio, alerting everyone there was an emergency. The dispatcher called my unit number and asked if my unit was ready to go. Whenever this happens, a crime is in progress with a possible suspect still on scene. In this case, it was a burglary. After I responded yes, I informed the dispatcher that I had a "rider" with me.

"Take it, Code 3," the dispatcher told me.

I flipped on the lights and siren, then took off. The "rider" looked at me with eyes wide as saucers and asked me if she had to go.

"Of course, you have to go!" I told her. "This is what I do! We don't get to pick and choose which crime we respond to!"

She didn't say another word. She held on for dear life as we sped to the location at a high rate of speed. I glanced over at her and noticed she was stiff as a board. She was literally trying to stop the car with both feet as she pressed her non-existent brakes. I thought she would press her feet straight through the car's floorboard. Stick a fork in her; she was done!

Prior to our arrival, the dispatcher gave an update saying the suspect was no longer on scene. I was relieved because I knew my "rider" wouldn't be able to handle another minute of my typical workday. At the completion of the call, my "rider" said she didn't want to finish the shift. No surprise there. I returned her to the police station, where her car was parked. I didn't run into her again until after I retired. She told me that she decided to open a group home instead of pursuing a career in law enforcement.

I couldn't help but laugh and tell her, "I think you made the right decision."

Wellness Checks

Uncle K.C. is the family favorite. The life of the party, he is loved by everyone, especially women. He was sixty-one years old chronologically but twenty-one mentally. He visited us often, always showing up with a hearty appetite and a different woman hanging on his arm. He introduced every single one of them to his nieces and nephews as our new "auntie."

In the early '80s, he lived in the downtown Toledo area. I worked out of the Central District Station, within walking distance of his house. Back then, downtown Toledo was alive with plenty of nightlife and "ladies of the evening ". My partner and I always checked on my uncle while heading to our district. When the weather permitted, he would hang outside with his buddies, but this day was different. It was summertime, and he wasn't on the front porch. When his front door is open, you can look straight through the house and see the back door. We saw two familiar "ladies "from the downtown area as we looked inside from the street. When they saw me, my partner, and our big paddy wagon, they fled out the back door and took off down the alley. We sat there laughing because they thought we would chase them on foot, but that wasn't necessary. We knew where to find them if we had to. My uncle came bursting through the front door. He was livid!

"Vicki, quit bringing your (expletive) ass by here!" he yelled.

This was the first and only time he didn't appreciate seeing me. Hey, I was just doing my job, which is "to protect and to serve". Those two Jezebels were no aunties of mine.

Reflections

As a nation, society, and people, we must ask ourselves: *Is this what God created us for? Is God pleased with our actions, or are we operating in selfishness?* To serve at your highest potential, you must take a hard look at yourself while asking the following questions:

- Am I being the best version of myself that I can be?

- What do I want the next generations' future to look like?

- How do I want our communities to be?

- What is the change I want for our children?

- What legacy will I leave for my children and future generations?

- What changes have I made within myself?

- What impact do I want to make in my community?

- Whose life will I impact?

- What lessons will I leave?

- How can I be the change needed by people?

- Am I a positive role model?

- What does unconditional love look like to me?

Conclusion

We hope something you read in this book touched your heart as it did ours. The events that occurred were real, and the women in the stories were up against real-life encounters. Policing was the start of something new for the ladies. From one day to the next, they didn't know what situations they would have to deal with or if they would even make it home at the end of their shift.

The Women in Blue memoir tells how women prevail in their careers despite the circumstances, controversies, and conflicts. Resilient since the beginning of time, women hold a significant role in many professions around the nation, especially law enforcement, and have strengths that amaze men. History shows that women have become the CEO of companies, Chiefs of Police, and Vice Presidents, to name a few positions of power. As time moves forward, there will be more and more women telling their stories of how we have prevailed, persevered, and pursued our purposes in life.

We thank you for supporting this project. May the blessings of the Lord be with you always!

14-DAY DEVOTIONAL
FOR A WOMAN'S
SOUL, SPIRIT, AND SANCTITY

14-DAY DEVOTIONAL

The last section of this book is a devotional. Our decision to include this was to show no matter who we are and where we are in life, everyone needs a break—a breather. Journaling can help with that. Use this devotional as a way to keep your thoughts in check. Setting aside time for journaling and devotion has kept us close to God and helps us move forward in life.

This 14-day devotional and meditation guide* will provide you with some insightful questions that will spark your thought process and get you thinking of ways in which you want to continue your own journey. The questions are meant to help us mentally, spiritually, and emotionally. We hope this will bless you in a mighty way as it did us. Remember, you are never alone in anything that you do. Enjoy!

*Scriptures are taken from the Bible Gateway's different interpretations. Scriptures in red are God speaking.

DAY ONE

How do you encourage yourself and give thanks for each day?

_____

_____

_____

_____

_____

_____

_____

_____

_____

_____

_____

_____

_____

_____

_____

_____

_____

_____

_____

_____

Scriptures for Reflection

I Chronicles 16:34 (KJV) O give thanks unto the Lord; for he is good; for his mercy endureth for ever.

Psalm 92:1 (KJV) It is a good thing to give thanks unto the Lord, and to sing praises unto thy name, O Most High.

I Corinthians 15:57 (KJV) But thanks be to God, which giveth us the victory through our Lord Jesus Christ.

Lamentations 3:22-24 (MSG) God's loyal love couldn't have run out, his merciful love couldn't have dried up. They're created new every morning. How great your faithfulness! I'm sticking with God (I say it over and over). He's all I've got left.

Romans 15:4 (AMP) For whatever was written in earlier times was written for our instruction, so that through endurance and the encouragement of the Scriptures we might have hope *and* overflow with confidence in His promises.

DAY TWO

How do you find help for yourself? How do you strengthen yourself?

_____

_____

_____

_____

_____

_____

_____

_____

_____

_____

_____

_____

_____

_____

_____

_____

Irene Reyes-Smith

Scriptures for Reflection

Isaiah 41:10 (KJV) Fear thou not; for I am with thee: be not dismayed; for I am thy God: I will strengthen thee; yea, I will help thee; yea, I will uphold thee with the right hand of my righteousness.

Psalm 28:7 (NKJV) The Lord *is* my strength and my shield; My heart trusted in Him, and I am helped; Therefore, my heart greatly rejoices, and with my song I will praise Him.

Psalms 27:1 (KJV) The Lord is my light and my salvation; whom shall, I fear? The Lord is the strength of my life; of whom shall I be afraid?

Matthew 6:32-33 (NLT) These things dominate the thoughts of unbelievers, but your heavenly Father already knows all your needs. Seek the Kingdom of God above all else, and live righteously, and he will give you everything you need.

DAY THREE

Do you have the patience to wait on the Lord?

_____

_____

_____

_____

_____

_____

_____

_____

_____

_____

_____

_____

_____

_____

_____

_____

_____

_____

_____

_____

Scriptures for Reflection

Psalms 27:14 (NKJV) Wait on the Lord; Be of good courage, And He shall strengthen your heart; Wait, I say, on the Lord!

Romans 5:3 (AMP) And not only *this,* but [with joy] let us exult in our sufferings *and* rejoice in our hardships, knowing that hardship (distress, pressure, trouble) produces patient endurance.

Hebrews 6:12 (AMP) so that you will not be [spiritually] sluggish, but [will instead be] imitators of those who through faith [lean on God with absolute trust and confidence in Him and in His power] and by patient endurance [even when suffering] are [now] inheriting the promises.

Matthew 6:34 (NLT) "So don't worry about tomorrow, for tomorrow will bring its own worries. Today's trouble is enough for today.

DAY FOUR

What is self-care to you? How do you execute it?

_____

_____

_____

_____

_____

_____

_____

_____

_____

_____

_____

_____

_____

_____

_____

_____

_____

_____

_____

_____

Irene Reyes-Smith

Scriptures for Reflection

Exodus 34:21 (AMP) You shall work for six days, but on the seventh day you shall rest; [even] in plowing time and in harvest you shall rest [on the Sabbath]

I Timothy 4:8 (NIV) For physical training is of some value, but godliness has value for all things, holding promise for both the present life and the life to come.

Proverbs 17:22 (AMP) A happy heart is good medicine *and* a joyful mind causes healing, but a broken spirit dries up the bones.

3 John 1:2 (NIV) Dear friend, I pray that you may enjoy good health and that all may go well with you, even as your soul is getting along well.

DAY FIVE

Did the pandemic make you wonder about your life, or did you continue life as usual?

_____

_____

_____

_____

_____

_____

_____

_____

_____

_____

_____

_____

_____

_____

_____

_____

_____

Scriptures for Reflection

Malachi 3:6 (CEV) Descendants of Jacob, I am the Lord All-Powerful, and I never change. That's why you haven't been wiped out.

Hebrews 13:8 (CEV) Jesus Christ never changes! He is the same yesterday, today, and forever.

II Corinthians 5:17 (AMP) Therefore if anyone is in Christ [that is, grafted in, joined to Him in faith in Him as Savior], *he is* a new creature [reborn and renewed by the Holy Spirit]; the old things [the previous moral and spiritual condition] have passed away. Behold, new things have come [because spiritual awakening brings a new life].

Psalm 91:10-12 (NLT) No evil will conquer you; no plaque will come near your home. For he will order his angels to protect you wherever you go. They will hold you up with their hands so you won't even hurt your foot on a stone.

DAY SIX

When struggles arise, do you seek God, family, or friends? What is your course of action?

Irene Reyes-Smith

Scriptures for Reflection

II Corinthians 1:5-6 (CSB) For just as the sufferings of Christ overflow to us, so also through Christ our comfort overflows. If we are afflicted, it is for your comfort and salvation. If we are comforted, it is for your comfort, which produces in your patient endurance of the same sufferings that we suffer.

Job 23:10 (HCSB) Yet He knows the way I have taken; when He has tested me, I will emerge as pure gold.

James 1:2-3 (AMP) Consider it nothing but joy, my brothers and sisters, whenever you fall into various trials. Be assured that the testing of your faith [through experience] produces endurance [leading to spiritual maturity, and inner peace].

Matthew 6:33 (AMP) But first *and* most importantly seek (aim at, strive after) His kingdom and His righteous [His way of doing and being right—the attitude and character of God], and all these things will be given to you also.

DAY SEVEN

Do you have an attitude of gratitude? What do you do when your attitude doesn't align with your spirit?

_____

_____

_____

_____

_____

_____

_____

_____

_____

_____

_____

_____

_____

_____

_____

_____

_____

_____

_____

_____

_____

Irene Reyes-Smith

Scriptures for Reflection

Psalm 106:1 (AMP) Praise the Lord! (Hallelujah!) Oh give thanks to the Lord, for He is good; For His mercy and loving kindness endure forever!

Philippians 4:4-6 (AMP) Rejoice in the Lord always [delight, take pleasure in Him]; again I say, rejoice! Let your gentle *spirit* [your graciousness, unselfishness, mercy, tolerance, and patience] be known to all people. The Lord is near. Do not be anxious or worried about anything, but in everything [every circumstance and situation] by prayer and petition with thanksgiving, continue to make your [specific] requests known to God.

I Thessalonians 5:18 (AMP) In every situation [no matter what the circumstances] be thankful *and* continually give thanks *to God*; for this is the will of God for you in Christ Jesus.

Hebrews 12:28 (AMP) Therefore, since we receive a kingdom which cannot be shaken, let us show gratitude, and offer to God pleasing service *and* acceptable worship with reverence and awe.

DAY EIGHT

What do you do when you feel your life's plan isn't lining up how you imagined it? Do you pray, or do you follow what the world is doing?

_____

_____

_____

_____

_____

_____

_____

_____

_____

_____

_____

_____

_____

_____

_____

_____

_____

Irene Reyes-Smith

Scriptures for Reflection

Jeremiah 29:11 (AMP) For I know the plans *and* thoughts that I have for you,' says the Lord, 'plans for peace *and* well-being and not for disaster, to give you a future and a hope.

Proverbs 16:3 (AMP) Commit your works to the Lord [submit and trust them to Him], And your plans will succeed [if you respond to His will and guidance].

I Peter 5:7 (AMP) Casting all your cares [all your anxieties, all your worries, and all your concerns, once and for all] on Him, for He cares about you [with deepest affection, and watches over you very carefully].

Matthew 6:33 (CEB) Instead, desire first and foremost God's kingdom and God's righteousness, and all these things will be given to you as well.

DAY NINE

Do you trust the path God has for your life? How do you seek the paths God has for your life?

_____

_____

_____

_____

_____

_____

_____

_____

_____

_____

_____

_____

_____

_____

_____

_____

_____

_____

_____

_____

_____

Scriptures for Reflection

Proverbs 16:20 (AMP) He who pays attention to the word [of God] will find good, and blessed (happy, prosperous, to be admired) is he who trusts [confidently] in the Lord.

Psalms 32:8 (AMP) I will instruct you and teach you in the way you should go; I will counsel you [who are willing to learn] with My eye upon you.

Psalms 25:4 (CSB) Make your ways known to me, Lord; teach me your paths.

I Kings 3:14 (MSG) And if you stay on course, keeping your eye on the life-map and the God-signs as your father David did, I'll also give you a long life.

DAY TEN

Do you seek God for His guidance? Do you show the same love to others as God shows you? Do you believe your life is aligned with God's will?

Scriptures for Reflection

John 15:12 (**AMP**) "This is My commandment, that you love *and* unselfishly seek the best for one another, just as I have loved you.

John 15:5 (AMP) I am the Vine; you are the branches. The one who remains in Me and I in him bears much fruit, for [otherwise] apart from Me [that is, cut off from vital union with Me] you can do nothing.

Ephesians 4:2 (AMP) with all humility [forsaking self-righteousness], and gentleness [maintaining self-control], with patience, bearing with one another in [unselfish] love.

I Chronicles 16:11 (CEB) Pursue the Lord and his strength; seek his face always!

Psalms 32:8 (NIV) I will instruct you and teach you in the way you should go; I will counsel you with my loving eye on you.

DAY ELEVEN

Do you do things out of desperation or follow God's word?

_____

_____

_____

_____

_____

_____

_____

_____

_____

_____

_____

_____

_____

_____

_____

_____

_____

_____

_____

Irene Reyes-Smith

Scriptures for Reflection

I Peter 5:6-7 (AMP) Therefore humble yourselves under the mighty hand of God [set aside self-righteous pride], so that He may exalt you [to a place of honor in His service] at the appropriate time, casting all your cares [all your anxieties, all your worries, and all your concerns, once and for all] on Him, for He cares about you [with deepest affection, and watches over you very carefully].

John 16:33 (AMP) I have told you these things, so that in Me you may have [perfect] peace. In the world you have tribulation *and* distress *and* suffering, but be courageous [be confident, be undaunted, be filled with joy]; I have overcome the world. "[My conquest is accomplished, My victory abiding.]

Psalm 37:3-5 (CSB) Trust in the Lord and do what is good; dwell in the land and live securely. Take delight in the Lord, and he will give you your heart's desires. Commit your way to the Lord; trust in him, and he will act

Proverbs 3:5-6 (CSB) Trust in the Lord with all your heart, and do not rely on your own understanding; in all your ways know him, and he will make your paths straight.

DAY TWELVE

How do you create the life that God created for you to live?

_____

_____

_____

_____

_____

_____

_____

_____

_____

_____

_____

_____

_____

_____

_____

_____

_____

_____

_____

_____

Scriptures for Reflection

Proverbs 19:21 (ESV) Many are the plans in the mind of a man, but it is the purpose of the Lord that will stand.

Proverbs 3:5-6 (AMP) Trust in *and* rely confidently on the Lord with all your heart And do not rely on your own insight *or* understanding. In all your ways know *and* acknowledge *and* recognize Him, And He will make your paths straight *and* smooth [removing obstacles that block your way].

Romans 12:2 (TLB) Don't copy the behavior and customs of this world, but be a new and different person with a fresh newness in all you do and think. Then you will learn from your own experience how his ways will really satisfy you.

Matthew 21:22 (NKJV) And whatever things you ask in prayer, believing, you will receive."

DAY THIRTEEN

Do you recognize the Lord's voice when he is speaking to you?

_____

_____

_____

_____

_____

_____

_____

_____

_____

_____

_____

_____

_____

_____

_____

_____

_____

_____

_____

_____

_____

Scriptures for Reflection

John 10:27 (TLB) My sheep recognize my voice, and I know them, and they follow me.

Revelation 3:20 (NIV) Here I am! I stand at the door and knock. If anyone hears my voice and opens the door, I will come in and eat with that person, and they with me.

Hebrews 2:1 (NIV) We must pay the most careful attention, therefore, to what we have heard, so that we do not drift away.

John 6:45 (MSG) This is what the prophets meant when they wrote, 'And then they will all be personally taught by God.' Anyone who has spent any time at all listening to the Father, really listening and therefore learning, comes to me to be taught personally—to see it with his own eyes, hear it with his own ears, from me, since I have it firsthand from the Father.

DAY FOURTEEN

Do you consider your home a place of peace? Or not?

_____

_____

_____

_____

_____

_____

_____

_____

_____

_____

_____

_____

_____

_____

_____

_____

_____

_____

_____

_____

Scriptures for Reflection

Psalm 4:8 (NIV) In peace I will lie down and sleep, for you alone, Lord, make me dwell in safety.

Romans 12:18 (TLB) Don't quarrel with anyone. Be at peace with everyone, just as much as possible.

2 Corinthians 13:11 (CSB) Finally, brothers and sisters, rejoice. Become mature, be encouraged, be of the same mind, be at peace, and the God of love and peace will be with you.

2 Thessalonians 3:16 (AMP) Now may the Lord of peace Himself grant you His peace at all times *and* in every way [that peace and spiritual well-being that comes to those who walk with Him, regardless of life's circumstances]. The Lord be with you all.